OF LIFE & OTHER S

OF LIFE
& OTHER SMALL SACRIFICES

The Selected Poems of
VLADIMIR AZAROV

Tiny Van Publishing

FIRST EDITION

copyright © Vladimir Azarov, 2010

All rights reserved. No part of this publication may be reproduced or transmitted in any form or by any means, electronic or mechanical, including photocopying, recording, or any information storage or retrieval system, without permission in writing from the publisher.

Cover Photogrpah by Vladimir Azarov
Edited for publication by Jay MillAr
Copy Edited by Amanda Hitchens

Distributed by LitDistCo: www.litdistco.ca and by Apollinaire's Bookshoppe: www.apollinaires.com

LIBRARY AND ARCHIVES CANADA CATALOGUING IN PUBLICATION

Azarov, Vladimir, 1935-
    Of life and other small sacrifices : selected poems / Vladimir Azarov.

ISBN 978-1-897388-74-7

    I. Title.

PS8601.Z37O45 2010   C811'.6   C2010-903862-2

TABLE OF CONTENTS

PART I. Prayer 12
Cirque 13
Game 14
An invitation 15
Silent 17
Mice 18
Sunset 20
Rain 21
Liner 22
Golden Silence 23
Monument 24
Moon 25
Walking 28
Subliminal 29
Fall 30
A Real Man 32
Sunbeam 33
Solipsism 35
Radio 37
Dada 38
Aria 39
A Shot 40
The War Requiem 43
Wave 48
Genius 49

PART II. A – Abstract 52
B – Balance 54
C – Crystal 55
D – Draught 56
E – Echo 57
G – Godiva 58
H – Homage 61
F – Forms 62
I – Icon 65
J – Jackie 66
K – Karenina 70
L – Library 71
M – Mayakovsky 72
N – Nude 74
O – Oliver 75
P – Picasso 77
Q – Quadruple 79
R – Reflection 80
S – Seven 81
T – Trinity 82
U – Unison 84
V – Verdict 86
W – Wave 87
X – Xioping 89
Y – You 90
Z – Zaha 91

PART III. The Early Morning Sun 94
Who's Afraid of My Plants? 95
O Hare! 100
O Rabbit Rabbit 101
The Fly Sleeps 102
The Mice 103
Octopus Stop! 104
Medusa You Are a Devil! 105
O Ox! 106
The Home Sphinx 107
Peacock Is Lifting 108
My Winged Pegasus 109
Parisian Flea 110
O Water Being Clone 111
You Dove 112
Hey Sirens 113
Bear in the Forest 114
A Quickly Running Lion 115
The Serpent Comes 116
A Plain Stray Dog Named Laika 117
Like Human Commuters 118
I Started Early 120
Behind the Door 124
The Man Dead 126
The Heat 127
A Knock 129
Two White Grey Birds 130
The Universe Seems Bankrupt 131
No Birds 133
Flying Away 134
I Watch a Birth of Song 135
The Monotonously Wide Frame 136
The Frosty Sky 139

Art is the lie that makes us realize truth.
– Pablo Picasso

PART I.

Life is tedious as a twice-told tale.
— William Shakespeare

PRAYER

give me one more happy minute
in my morning window's light
a blue and beaming beautiful
or glad glum gloomy sky
above an uneven line of walls
before the random walkers of the morning
pass with their squatting dogs
then stoop with plastic bags

give me another happy minute
with the sound of this morning's
fizz whiz breath of the grinding
coffee maker

CIRQUE

a tent-wooden Circus Cart creaks under the many
goods & sundries – the steaming road-dust tail

sways to the slow and rhythmic clatter of horse shoes
now look at the riders – a bendable boy with a hint of horns

plays the pipe – he straddles the front seat as he plays
from behind a curtain a disgruntled old woman peers out

and behind her a circus monkey and a pale baby's crying face
a pony-tailed girl jumps from the cart precisely

and pirouettes into the morning air – she runs to the bushes –
nature calls – she hides from all lost knights and curious onlookers

afterwards she stands and stops – she sees the four ends of this poem:

1)
the circus-monkey sits by the horned boy embracing the baby
sucking on a stale cloth-covered hunk of bread –

2)
the old woman turns to the girl and spit – "in two hundred years
just offspring will witness a miracle called Cirque du Soleil!"

3)
in the full-length mirror a girl admires her vertical leg
a horned boy holds for her a large ball that says – "Cirque du Soleil"

4)
Picasso's "The Circus Cart" hangs on the hotel room wall
In plain sight of the woman's child who stars – wide-eyed

GAME

> *Everything led into primal knowledge.*
> – H. Hesse, The Glass Bead Game

try to catch them
my rolling
cold glass beads
that spill across the floor
I want to gather them
but they scatter and flee
these untouchable spheres
short lived and featureless
evading
dodging
their obstacles is me
playing this untitled game
with shiny pellets
that perpetually spill away
and I am a sighing man

AN INVITATION

   hey
come out for a shot of vodka from my not quite
empty bottle of *Stolichnaya* – it will relieve our boredom
and our loneliness
come in the early evening
say between 6:00 and 6:30
   it's so convenient – I live near King station –
   come and see my narrow room with its unwashed
big wide window   look at my
tight downtown yard lacking sunshine
   inside the tall boring walls
are a couple of ever-semi-green fir trees
   beside their bending shaking birch brothers
on the parkette-top
of the parking lot
a remembrance of nature
and we will listen to music on the radio
   music with long speeches before and after
the kind they play on Saturdays at 1:00
the live Metropolitan opera
Verdi's *Rigoletto* for example
separated by long conversations
   intervals washed down with either
finely ground decaffeinated coffee from the drugstore
on the corner of Yonge and King
   or not-so-strong milky tea
and whole-grain crackers (5% fat)

   but if
you aren't here because either I have
not invited you or you are too busy
I will sit alone and wait for

   the raining lull of the rhythm-drops that sound
through the slightly open window to accompany
the lulling rhythms of FM 94.1
and think of your ill temper
   your treacherous perilous disposition

SILENT

suddenly it falls silent
all four elements are still
the restless waves of a stormy life are gone
everything falls asleep in an instant

the palpable and pulsing dreams
swing in suspense – thank goodness for magnetism
lamented in an unpredictable
trance waving fate

sighs penetrate
into the self
invented destination
piercing an empty

silhouette of flat glass
we await the dark night's tide

MANHATTAN MICE

about 20 years ago I took a very cheap trip
to New York – it was my fondest dream to visit Manhattan
my old friend Yuri asked me to take $400
for the daughter of his co-worker Marina – I remember
Yuri and I dropped in on this lady's place – her then
16-year-old daughter Alyona blasted in on us – a t-shirt and
short wearing Moscow teenager speaking slang and coursing
but o! breathtaking Manhattan! Even my window faces
the Empire State Building – I stay in a semi-clean Arabian hotel
with dirty narrow wooden stairs and breath in
the cosmopolitan air – I call Alyona – hear her new
not-Moscow voice on the phone – I get ready pocket –
the & 400 and run down to meet her the lobby is empty
except for a darkly dressed old woman who sits alone
suddenly she runs to me cries 'Mr. Vladimir!'
and hugs me – it's her! – the lurking cursing girl
of my memories! What happened? Her mother failed
to tell me that her daughter had crossed the ocean as a
Hasidic bride to live in this shining cosmos space city – she
wears a wig of ugly artificial hair and glum unfashionable
clothes – I feel so sorry! but to my surprise she is sorry for me!
'Mr. Vladimir' – she asks – 'why did you come to this ugly
glass metal jungle? how I miss our beautiful gold headed
Moscow' – we talk – I give her the $400 – she has brought
me two heavy bags filled with Hasidic kosher food

that night I wake to a strange sound loud and rustling
the Manhattan mice are after Alyona's tasty smelling bags!
I hit the light – mice scatter in every direction! What am I to do?
I hang the bags from the old-fashioned chandelier and try to
sleep again – but I can't – the mice persist with their hasty scratch
scratching – opening eyes I see them dancing leaping to reach

the tempting bags alight in the Manhattan neon lights –
outside my window – the Empire State Building's silhouette
peeks in and whispers a New York admonition –
'the Manhattan mice do not sleep at night completely'

SUNSET

before the night the sun of the sunset
elbows light to a different semi-sphere
struggles down through the clouds' rows
that change the sun's gowns gradually –
lemon bright above the treetops
something orange caught between branches
an agony of red crushed by density
resisting layers of cloud at the horizon

RAIN

the warm fat drops of rain
leaping on one leg as a jumping girl
changing legs quickly –
left right – right left

trying to leap over all obstacles
but sliding-falling
spilling with flashes on the green grass
the stubborn leaves of grass – attempting to avoid

the overwhelming moisture
bending slipping away
tired shivering irritably
eyed diamond wink twinkling

beneath the limp one-legged fat drops
of the warm summer rain

LINER

Eight Tattered Scraps of Paper from my Pocket

"nature has painted this landscape."
(Cruise Ship Journal – Saturday, August 5th, 2006)
an ocean liner heads for gold-iced
Alaska – my childhood dream of Jack London's tales, of ice and
snow, the husky sledge – goodbye Seattle! Hello – o my Alaskan
dreams!
a shocking nautical luxury – gourmet meals 24 hours
a day on every deck – comfort-lounges from "an affair
to remember" shining spas for everyone! "art auction" –
3:15 and every night at 6:00: "main sitting gala dinner"
 with friends –
the sitters and walkers of all decks' wooden floors –
young full-mouthed barefoot dancers, sporty semi-naked wet
jogging runners, grey respectably dressed men, head-covered seriously
walking Hasids with their kids –
this sailing white Giant,
population: 2000 – sailing the silver iceberg waves rimmed by
the grass and snow of mountainous silhouettes of Hollywood-bright
towns – the splash of a dolphin's playful escort – the jet-steam tail –
the tanning flocks of pony-tailed aging ladies, their open necks
on open desks.
a Northern Happiness – until two days in – the ocean
unpleasantly rolls and a Titanic complex rises
the sadly melting
glaciers cry with bitter tears into the salty ocean mourning Global
Warming, & perhaps over a former Russian territory – 1867 –
7 200 000 humorous buckskins – Alaska's prize!
today, no
Russian nostalgia – the Russian Church in Juneau stands empty.
the old Russian names are cast temporarily in the yellow pages just
as in Alaska's wild subconscious memory

IN GOLDEN SILENCE

my life's duet:
a tenuous knowledge
of language
and
my silent quest
for English verse –
I am not emotional
I am disciplined obedient.
I need the exact phrase
but
my dark ignorance
of the shades of words unties
my hands my tongue
my thoughts my feelings
even my words
are out of place
the childish freedom
the longing of an infant poet

my pen pulls to the paper

a stream of semi-known words
that pour and rush
and dart forward
like mad horses who start
with a jerk to dash across
the endless
steppes   prairies   countries
leaving me in a wonderland
of golden silence

MONUMENT
for Glen Gould's 75th Birthday

Mount Pleasant greens are solitary, green
and peaceful – his solitude continues
beneath the stone where his body lies.
A sunny warm September – he is 75
we come to him.
He is already many years in this green Heaven
with birds and their songs
his gentle stormy piano J.S. Bach accompanied
by leaves' trees music rain's drops drums
a wind whirl thunderstorm's orchestra.
We need him amid us in town
downtown – we need an encounter again –
he was invisible for many years
before his is untimely time,
we miss him – our Glen Gould.
O! but be more attentive!
do you see him? – Glen Gould!
not his modest stone at Mount Pleasant,
but here – down town!
He sits on the plain street bench
on Front Street
in front of this big Musical CBC building –
alive again but slightly embarrassed and smiling,
behind him –
his great Bach monumental wall
Glen Gould is bronze, but he live casually
turns to talk to you, to me, to passing Torontonians,
to a girl who wants to take a picture
instead of the autograph
that her grandmother has

MOON
for Thomas

the starlit night of the early spring.
the bright full Moon
looked at my friend & I
softly peacefully with a deep curiosity,
widely opened its eyes like
a pregnant woman,
embracing the dark-blue sky-universe
with its whispering trembling halo – steamy
as our breathing mouths
we stared back at it attentively
my friend –
'*I see the tiny-tiny spots in it.*'
I –
'*Which spots?*'
he continued – '*the dark
& tiny ones. We can see just the Sun's
reflection, but not the Moon itself.
the light from the starlit Stars
takes years to reach us, essentially*'
flashing
with his eyes
'*also from the Moon.
If somebody came from the Stars to our Earth,
we would see him still at his Star*'
his smiling face, paled by
the Moon, was fulfilled.
'*really?*'
I, vacantly. Coming to my senses –
the light speed – 300 000 km per second,
the Moon so close. My light irony –
'*aha!*

*Now you see the footprint-image of Mr.
Armstrong – maybe? But he returned
to his Cincinnati University
long ago*

*I have a witness – a relative of,
mine – she was visited by this space-man
at her Cincinnati school. Neil –
a retired astronaut –
this spring evening (warm enough
in Cincinnati)
timely' – I saw my wrist –
'after eight, –
I'm sure – he's drinking his
garden milk-tea with his wife
& candy –
After-Eight –
looking at his Moon-trace
through his domestic
telescope at space –
at his sticky-walking Moon-body
poor, there non-existent-now body
wrong – on the hilly Moon,
still thirsts for a real cup of tea'
'o! such
a lively cosmos-picture' –*
my friend's excited voice
enjoying our fantastical mind-nonsense,
our ignorance
*'today's a dream –
tomorrow is reality'*

his widely opened eyes were
two big full moons

& his open steaming mouth
supplied his thrilling breath

the bright but already sleepy Moon
confused completely,
looked at us respectfully –
but with a curious surprise
and an alien compliment

WALKING
After W. H. Auden

as I am walking along Yonge street
    I'm glad to see this urban space –
the hugging prisms' high buildings meet
    a walking man's surprising face

I'm new in town and in a walking mood,
    I like this live glass stone walk
by Eaton's moving ocean I am lured –
    I like this buzzing crowd's talk.

Roy Thompson-Hall is my temptation –
    under tune music I am again
like geese in sky – imagination
    embracing me – a walking man.

this call depicts a real spring
    a green grass valley and a splashing lake
a suntanned hero as the kith and kin
    smiles blessing mighty – "hey! wake!

a walking man! this ringing bell for you!
    this warming sun and sand's footprint!
be young again! Enjoy this view!"
    I'm glad – but stop! I hear a ticking hint –

the sand just burns – a song is missed –
    nobody conquers the seasons' break!
street window mirrors a lit watch wrist –
    beneath high sky – above deep lake

SUBLIMINAL
After Deirdre Logue's Video 'Beyond Her Usual Limits'

my bathroom is tight –
not enough room for dancing
after my morning shower-shaving about 7:30
i like to waltz-turn to the music reaching me from my living room
my radio 96.3
my lazy exercise.
once –
in a flash (i'm already shaving)
my flashing glance unexpectedly catches
a stopped mirror image
i'm shocked i continue
to turn afraid of teasing a phenomenon
i feel my frozen echo notices my bug-eyed look
i carefully stop my optic twin's confused face
looks at me as an apology might
because i caught his eye
               what is it?
a cryptic effect of the 25th frame?
my quick materialistic speculation?
what else? what do i need to do?
search again this morse code?
spin on?
the broken down reparation?
i have a scary hesitation
please stop me from this search
a secret puzzle doesn't have an open
reparation preparation
like an environmental brown paper bag
if it's well-worn with holes
it cannot be blown again
it doesn't have new real life

FALL

        I like

to forest trees
    the soft

with red-gold leaves
    I hear

of singing blooms
    this windy

the forest rooms
    the fall

love very much –
    so light

I like to touch
    my crimson

to walk
and talk

land bed
is spread

the crunchy
bunches

song
along

drink-wood
I should

to breathe,
& leaves –

path
dry grass –

the road to fly
    the weak   sunbeam –
                            a dream

in changing sky
    the sun   will hide
                            behind

the heavy cloud
    an uncovered   head
                            is wet

the autumn proud
    it will   soon rain
                            again

he cold will rise
    the water   drop
                            will stop –

as crystal ice

A REAL MAN
A Paired-Line Sonnet to a Real Man

a real Man's every-morning essence
o! his slightly stretched strong toned muscles

the humming morning-satisfied robed wife
(or a girl-friend or – maybe somebody else)

gladly pouring the black brewed hot coffee
making noise with the china cups mugs plates

stirring the hissing yellow-bubbled scramble
unwrapping cutting cold supermarket food

o! the sniffing flashing man's sink-water joy
then the bathroom's Hugo Boss unstable smell

the rustling new many-paged coloured news
the strong-brewed black coffee's hurried gulp

the glad sunbeam plays on the kitchen table
the real Man's every morning essence

SUNBEAM

1

i am a boy – a winter window
with sunny crisp frost – morning
a forest of patterned ice & glass
a sunbeam peeking into the window
tickling my still sleepy face
smiling elbowing inside making room
the wet sill weak frost in
the morning sun bright but veiled view
eyes hurt to look at the shining snow
no class today just warm & cozy at home
where is my sunbeam my running beam?
i turn – the shadow of frost against
the back wall plays on the carved board
dancing winking friendly at me – a boy

2

i'm looking at the window   again
i drink (O) the sunny window's light
i squint – an enjoyable warmth warms
i'm glad to hug (O) this morning at home
i spin I giggle quietly (!O!) 9:30
i'm sitting at the after-eating table
(tomorrow will be my serious math test
i need my usual mark – my 'excellent')
looking at my textbook
the playful   (O) beam above my head
the hanging (O) trembling shining shaft
not disturbing warmly brushing
my still uncombed disheveled hair
still creased from my night pillow

SOLIPSISM

i
am a real kid i see my face in the glass-mirror
i am cheek-touchable with my small fingers
but i can touch kiss lick the glass
and see my animation simultaneously
two baby boys – me plus my reflection
but if i close my eyes – we both disappear
i & my mirror twin – where are we? haloo!

i
am a schoolboy then i'm a student with smart ideas
the term 'SOLIPSISM'
i knew it when i was only five
i told the teacher it is NOTHING if i don't see it
all – I YOU THEY – are the real selves are a reality
but all around us exists unreal decoration –
all that we see – sky – lake – ocean – wood
sport play war business love our joy or sadness
are just the eye brain sense skin's echo – reflection

i
look into the mirror
i see the female lines of the same person
my girl my fiancée my wife & someone else
i'm scared & i quickly close my eyes
o! i am no boyfriend no fiancé no husband!

i
am a SOLIPSIST – it means an optimist
i am so happy & free i am alive again
when i close my eyes –
i am what i want – so easy my reflected world!

what's that i – you say – an egotist? an egoist?
o no no no no!

i
am a SOLIPSIST – – – a solipsist forever!

RADIO

> *Hearty kisses.*
> *In a minute.*
> *Shut the door.*
>   – Gertrude Stein

I'm a small boy –
    it's ww ii – my family lives out in the sticks
in a Kazakhstan coal town called Karaganda.
    a hanging radio that looks like a black paper plate
is my only entertainment – music – words
    from the small town broadcasting station

once, there was suddenly a
    woman's loud voice in my speaker –
"shut the door!"
    then, more powerfully – "do you hear me?
hey! shut the door!"

    o! my door is open!
tip-toeing very quietly
    I come down and shut the door
I hear the squeak of the closing door
    from my all seen radio

DADA

my early painting passion
        I'm ten
my fantasy of hard times
        oh! it's impossible to buy the tube-oil-colours
oh? oil? I'll use some cooking oil
        boil it with a colophony for quick-drying
colours? I use the fine green powder
        a tree-insects' bad killer
romantically called 'Parisian Green', my green
        I mix it with my alchemist boil-fry-oil
the red?
        I have the red-roof-paint's colour lead
o thus I have art-painted colourful oil-pictures
        the bright-kitsch copies
of my grandmother's pre-revolution cards
        by suburb train I go to the market
to exchange my Dada-folk-art-products
        for melting rose ice-cream
but Dadaism's sold secret from my parents

ARIA

i'm squeaking an aria in a young boy's voice
        along
with the spinning vinyl
        on a plastic
old-fashioned gramophone
        smelling of leather
the shining curved hand with its short needle
        produces a sound
for my experiment in Karaoke
        my descant duet with Rigoletto's Duke
and a pioneer of recorded music
        Caruso or Bolshoi's tenor Lemeshev
before the mirror I try to stick
        my shaggy head into a paper envelope's
round narrow hole – to make
        a Duke's horizontal collar
sadly it is not pleated

A SHOT
for my childhood

PART ONE

I am a small boy – a spectator
At the amateur labour club performance
My father on the stage
Plays a "white" tsar officer
Wearing his dark navy student jacket
With straps of cardboard on his shoulders
Some Russian Revolution play from
The Moscow Art Theatre's repertoire
I hardly recognize my father's pale white face
A shot rings out! – my father falls
I cry in my loud boy's voice
My mother brings me backstage
To the softly smiling actresses
And my smiling father
I weep & go to the foyer
To look for a washroom

PART TWO

> *All animal are equal but some animal*
> *are more equal than others.*
> — George Orwell

But with my adult curiosity
I see among red slogans on the wall
A huge striped monster portrait
I wonder at the canvas
Caged by vertical strips glued perpendicularly
I stand in front of this ribbed Sphinx
And bold Lenin's purple look
Looks at me from this modernist icon
But if I go left I see the stripes' left side
With moustached Stalin's painted green face!
Such a tricky game to me!
I go right & check the right view
This painted striped perspective shows me
Marx's red-bearded portrait
O! I liked this tree-coloured zoo cage
With the well-known faces

(O! but I won't be acquainted with
The already jailed or killed
Surrealist or Dada or Futurist artists
But by Leon Trotsky manifested
With French Poet Andre Breton
And this striped triptych was the rest
of that still art-free time)

But I have two topical smart questions:
Where is Engels? The fourth face?
I remember him from my Kindergarten's wall

He is a constant member
Of this quartet
And why does this powerful "Red" colour belong
Not to Leader Stalin?

THE WAR REQUIEM
for Galina Vishnevskaya

*Everyone who hates his brother is a
murderer & you know that no murderer
has eternal life in him.*
— John 3:15

Prologue)   the early 1970s – I listened to *The
War Requiem* by Britten with the
Russian star soprano Vishnevskaya –
a great performance and a howling
success in Moscow – then a coincidence –
soon I went to England – came to historical
Coventry (a contemporary sample
of a demographic
'satellite' of London) not knowing the strong
connection of this town with my recently
listening to Britten's *Requiem*

Coventry's Mayor
turning his empty pockets out, saying – 'alas,
no restaurant just coffee dear guests' – then
giving us a hint –
'do not miss our Cathedral'

the coffee was excellent.

1)   I stood in front of St. Michael's
cathedral, rebuilt as a memorial of WW II –
the scenic old church in ruins now, the rich
history, mentioning Lady Godiva,
& near – a new post-modern stylized Cathedral.
breath-taking spring-sunny holy view...

1940 – the air-raids – the Blitz.
Coventry was cruelly bombed – then – 1943
British Coventry & Russian Stalingrad
became 'the Twinned-Towns' after the crucial
Stalingrad battle destroyed the Russian city totally.
two wiped out towns unhappy manly brothers –

2)   1940 – the composer left London
during the bomb attacks . At first to Canada,
then to the USA – he followed the British
poet W. H. Auden for collaboration
in their pacifist mission – but Britten's soul stayed
in England
after War time – still not forgetting
his absence from his Home during the War
the composer ran to his solemn memorial
tribute – the War with its victims
1958 – Sir Benjamin
Britten was commissioned to write the Mass
for the consecration of St. Micheal's – birth of the 1960s
Britten's music was almost ready – he gave the part
of the lead Mourner – as all soldiers' Mother –
to a Russian singer as the 'twinned brothers'
representative! o! the composer needed to meet his
chosen soprano – Vishnevskaya – the Mass was
written for her – o! far-off mysterious country Russia!
Britten needed to show his new war-work to his friend
the Russian great composer Dmitri Shostakovitch.

3)   go-ahead spirits! by car! go ahead
through Europe! foreseeing the travel difficulties –
the destroyed roads & a shortage of fuel
but go ahead. Driving from Suffolk with his close friend
Peter Pears a tenor from the Mass – driving through

Cambridge Oxford et cetera – in London parting.
then across Europe seeing the War's
traces – after fortunate Belgium –
so many German cities crushed, or wept completely
the ancient from the Holy Roman Empire –
Cologne – now a no-stone re-building city
just following the old streets' contour
and just two well-known majestic Gothic heads
what will be awaiting these sophisticated
UK members of musical Good Will –
in Russia? o! long Russian four
year's war! still-destroyed settlements & towns...

4)   a Hotel near
the Kremlin. Britten in Moscow! he saw a few
men in the roomy lobby & a woman.
o! the Mourner- Mother! star
Vishnevskaya!
Britten was stunned – an elegant
and very slim attractive woman – no typical Opera Diva
friendly smiling with white roses in her welcome –
outstretched hands

5)   the Mess of victims of senseless
murders, of men, history's hostages –
grandfather-fathers, husband-grooms, young man-boys

'What passing bell for these who die as cattle?'

Britten's English mind remembered his
beloved compatriot Poet of the First World War –
Wilfred Owen – killed at only 25 – o! Britten's
real dream – it will be soon –
in May 1962,

The War Requiem premiere – the bright lights
in the trembling night air; the starlit sky of the
spring chilly evening. Applause – the composer among
his friends & all the World
the lit slightly-
steaming real setting – a new St. Michael
and the Sacred Ruins – the Mass background.
the geometrically divided space for
many many singers – 'soldiers'
the former enemies – now friends

'I'm the enemy you killed, my friend.
Let us sleep now…'

the Latin Mass for a new Cathedral.
and the Mother Mourner sang & prayed for
both sides' soldiers-victims in her strong
powerful soprano – soldiers obeying
this magic lulling voice!

Epilogue)   o! it was the composer's
dream. He dreamed it many times…
however the composer still didn't
know – his divine soprano
would be prevented from standing
'next to
a German & an Englishman
performing a political work'
 yes, prevented by the Soviet Government –
to sing with the West-different camp-singers
a political piece!
the visible '*hot*' War
was finished in 1945, a hidden '*cold*' –
continued

the May Mass grand-performance
was held without the Russian singer Galina –
the mother mourner
o! so dramatically she was
replaced by another singer! Poor Britten!
Just the next year, recording for the World,
Vishnevskaya sang in Latin –
Sir Benjamin Britten's War-Mass –

'Lord, grant them eternal rest, & let
the perpetual light shine upon them.'

'Let them rest in peace'…

WAVE

my wave
the water waving element on edge
embraces me with soft bubble foam
kisses me with waving restless salty lips
the sighing hard-breathing swollen phantom
a flood with sparkle crests
of the whirl-whipped splash spun dance
of my wave waving
we're waving both – we are alone
we wave among the waves
beneath the sleeping sky
we're both breathing hard with ticking hearts

o wayward wave!
do not deprive me of my late dream!
as my last dream drowned
in depths you gave
o my own waving wave
one of the many waves
but my own!
waving me do not wrap around my head
o my only wave! one of the many waves
you cannot save? run me aground

o my dear wave! be my last chance

GENIUS

> *'Everything you can imagine is real.'*
> – Pablo Picasso

    I am a genius

    do not kill me
    like Salieri Mozart!
    do not hunt me
    because
    I am a genius

do not set on me
    the Black Lady
    with her scythe

I do not like her
    Because
    instead
of plaited plaits
    or
the tied babushka
of an old-fashioned lady
she wears a hood
    upon
her shining void round
cracked bone skull
    I hate it

o! save me!

    I am a genius!

PART II.

When words are scarce, they are seldom spent in vain.
– William Shakespeare

ABSTRACT
for Black Square

A Square is a grown Point!
The line is a set or multitude of points dots spots
Pulled to the left & right! Yes! The first dimension
Of the   pouring creek of points!
O but   if you can grasp one of these many
Points   (the cell or atom of the line)
Don't   splash the line & pull it (the point)
O! so   carefully even to the north east
South west in four directions!
                 Look!
Do you see a transformation? You gave birth to the Square
The second plain dimension!
The pure Square was born!
For what? Go farther! Now grasp the Square! It's easy
Then take out! Hold it! Kazimir Malevich
Could do it very easily & he transformed the Square
Into the embryo of art-abstract then into the famous
Russian geometric Art Suprematism! The Square! The smallest
Part of life! The pixel of the canvas screen! Malevich as a
Painter needed the painted   multiplying squares!
                .Look!
This   Black Square on this   white background!
But it could be White or Red – the Background or the Square!
The Black Square is the old oil-brush Monument of the new
Era painting from Microcosm Square to Macrocosm's Abstract
Complex & tangled   brushed nonobjective actions!
          O! I've got it!
Malevich's Squares are the same as the Points of the French
Pointillism of Georges Seurat!
     However!
Do not confuse Malevich's strong geometric method

with Chagall's soft-soul – they both worked in the small Russian town Vitebsk – the womb of the famous Russian avant-garde! Long live the Black Square!

BALANCE

I am not Vladimir Nabokov I am not famous
Not a celebrity not a novelist historian or critic
I will not finish my life at the Montreux Palace Hotel
We were born in the same city, St Petersburg
We are namesakes and our sons share the same names
And we both come to North America from Russia
But I am not Nabokov I began to learn English
Very recently I did not grow up among Russian
Anglophones my father was not an aristocrat was
Not killed in Berlin by the Tsar's protagonists
The Russian white right wing Nabokov's father
Was not a student arrested in Leningrad-St Petersberg
By the red communist left wing I've neither caught
A butterfly nor liked teenage girls I was never
Obsessed with chess I hate chess I do not have a
Gay brother who was killed by the Nazis nor
A Jewish wife

           Nabokov is my
Incitement to comprehend my new language he
Shows me his sterile literary space and his
Talent makes 'art for art' his stream of art more
Naturally convincing than our real life and his
Intricate allusions pour in a flow of words a magic
Carpet of the human mind and dreams mean more
Than life itself but nevertheless I am not
Vladimir Nabokov not completely

CRYSTAL

Cities are the greatest creations of humanity.
— Daniel Libeskind

o CRYSTAL! o my love!
instead of the tall boring glass pillars of condos
we see you: a fresh art-shaped existence for our
city with a modern architectural experience
from Mies van der Rohe

o CRYSTAL! o my love!
the erected shining pyramids — memorabilia of history & culture!
eventually a modern blow to the monotonous linear streets!
the excited Toronto crowd runs to your grand unveiling!

o CRYSTAL! listen to this ticket-holder's showy voice:
"our patriarch — the grey Earl ROM with noble name —
your Art-Deco or Beaux-Arts now has a marginal alliance with a
flirting girl's circus equestrienne — Deconstruction"

o CRYSTAL! — "we need a fresh artistic wind in our loving city!" —
the next mind following history's run follows the evolution-revolution
the Pyramid-Mars-hint or tangled-Galaxy-footprint
the ROM's gigantic thousand-vertebra stegosaurus inclining its
head shows the art-huge historically-grown knife-teeth
to the frightened ticket-holder: "what is it? Beaux-Arts?
Secession? or Avant-Garde?"

o CRYSTAL! o my love!
instead of the boring downtown glass-pillars we see you
o crystal CRYSTAL!

DRAUGHT
Listening to Jon's Music

the rain drops' hail balls drum beat
the punk-leap ballet-running barefoot young couple – girl-boy
the open window's wind with the agile snaky draught
the techno-blasting open door
the whiz-whistle whispering of all-elements
                         ///////////////////////////
the rain drops' fat flat hit beat drum drop   //////////
drops   /// ///////////////////////////////
the slash flashing noise   //////// /////////////////////////////////
of the pouring shower   ///////////////////////////
or open water pipes   ///////////////////////////// ///////////////
the endless loud-rough-   ////////// /// //// //////////////////////
rustle-falling water wall   ////// ////////// //////////////// //////////////
the whirl of   ///////////////////////////// //////////// //// ////////////////
petal fang horn feather   ///////////////// //////////////
transforming   //////////////////////////////////////
into the hailing rhythmic tap rap   ////////////// /
the small balls' drum or   //////// //////////////
fingers' beat knock talk pour-penetrating   //////////////
techno no-tech   /////////////////////////
nature's extreme stream through the   ////////////
soaked transparent couple's shirts   //////////
on the couple's curve-bending backs   ////////////// //
the leap-flash running barefoot young couple
girl-boy   ////////////   girl-boy   ////   //////////////
    girl-boy   //////////////////
now beneath the flashing shy sun-light
the sun peeks from the torn waltz-swirling clouds
"the blind rain" it's called in Russia if it's a sunny rain
i'd like to know the local term but girl & boy still run
beneath my new bawl-loud techno-motto after the
soft cotton clouds – listen to the classic music

ECHO

> *What can I say?*
> *It comes & goes*
>   – Joni Mitchell

o! travelling travelling travelling
with a singing echo as a Symphony

o Joni's songs her music & her poem-lyrics
o the inhuman haunting dissolving sounds
of a woman's gentle voice
the wave-transparent vibrant sounds
hanging in the atmosphere sharp & penetrating
into the endless wild nature
of a roadless northern landscape
north of her Saskatoon of bridges
back to the dense urban stone jungles
of the North-American environmental cities
into the already ancient world of the sixties
the immortal days of rock'n roll
her blue blooming bloom that travels from yesterday
to now from man to woman from woman to man
from nature to human being
who tastes the sweet love travelling
through the nothingness that lasts so long
the singing ringing bell
the trembling notes
the flooding silver vocals
opera jazz country bouquet of
refined frost-fragrant flowers

o! travelling travelling travelling
songs sound as a Symphony

GODIVA

> *Mount your horse & ride naked,*
> *before all the people through the*
> *market of this town from one*
> *end to the another.'*
>   – Roger of Wendover, Chronic

clippity-clop – clop, clop, clop
I hear this very far but very real sound
I stand in front of Coventry's
landmark – I see the ruins of the ancient
church – bombed by the 'Coventry Blitz'
in 1940 & its neighbour – a new Cathedral built
by the modern architect Sir Basil Spence –
o! the unusual English May –
the bright romantic sunny day –
the history! I hear the clatter of a horse's hooves
a hoof-beat sounds hollowly upon
the cobbled street in the Anglo-Saxon
Mercia main town – Coventry – the early
evening – about 1000 (!) years ago – the slowly
stepping obedient respectful horse-hooves
clippity-clop –

our guide sighs softly smiling

the beautiful female figure riding
completely naked just covered
by her long blond hair –
two maids on horseback flanked her –
the famous riding Legend of Coventry
Lady Godiva

The guide looks at us with shining eyes

clippity-clop –
a folk-loving Lady Godiva
the wife of the ruler Leofric
in Coventry she founded a nunnery
the school the church of her Savior St. Mary
later St. Michael's – today in ruins –

The guide points to the ash-pearl ruins

a warrior – the powerful Leofric –
eventually – with an empty public purse –
o! his beautiful wife's blame – then –
the Earl's huge taxes – the big bad tribute –
o! why such an expensive church? explain
Lady Godiva – your task –
to free the folk at any cost – o Lady Godiva!
Our guide continues with her sad face
the inventive Leofric offers the Lady
(so beautiful & sporting) an interesting condition –
to show the now poor villagers her true naked beauty
as a Greek or Roman Goddess or our
first Lady Eve – then he promises to remove
the taxes except the horse levy
o! clop, clop, clop –
the Lady was religious & ashamed – but for the sake of
her folk – she agreed to her brave march! her horseback crusade
clop, clop, clop –
the early evening – all though her respectful townspeople
stayed behind closed doors – at the Lady's request
clop, clop, clop

The guide: you've heard about 'peeping Tom'?

Lady Godiva was seen by the town tailor young Tom
who couldn't resist a peek from between his wood shutters
at the naked beauty – so handy for peeping Tom
the very narrow medieval streets –
for voyeuristic happiness – o! voyeuristic sin!
(the feedback of the Noble Lady's exhibitionist provocation?)
poor Tom was blinded instantly –
but clop clop clop
(the Great Event needs some victims)
yes! clippity-clop clop clop

The lady-guide's conclusion:
the English Heroine still rides today at the Godiva
Festival – come on July! – o! sorry! – lunch time!
we go to the restaurant 'Lady Godiva'!

clop, clop, clop – clipity clop
I hear this very far but very real sound
and echo –
clop, clop, clop – clipity clop

clop, clop, clop – clipity
clop, clop, clop –
clop, clop,
clop

HOMAGE

I embraced a cloud,
but when I soared
it rained.
          – Frank O'Hara

i've never walked along the Sandbank of Fire Island
i've never seen blond Lana Turner on a screen
i've never listened to the blue Prokofiev-Scriabin chords
played by Frank O'Hara – a pianist, a dominant in poetry
but I discover him – a poet who went on nerve, he lived in poems
i hear his Verse-Voice resonate from myth-mysterious Manhattan
the time of his *Lunch-Poems* with the *yellow helmets* or *Jackson Pollock*
or with his Blue-Muse collapsing from too much living
in Hollywood it never snows, *there is no rain in California*
it's hailing in New York – a neon patch on his artistic Roman nose
changed by the dark & tragic signal *memento mori* – the Fire Land's
sand-whirl blows waving MOMA's façade-flagged flag

the broken Steinway sound-string hangs in the air
a stopped stanza's line hung in the grave silence

FORMS

for Moore's Collection at the AGO

I

I looked at Henry Moore, a tall majestic
man, & his granite marble concrete wood,
bronze streamlined living aliens – imposing clouds
landing in his lab, a garden near London –
Much-Hadham.
I've landed too – on a foggy
rainy UK planet. May drizzle, the seventies. The sculptor's
measured steps, & we follow him
art-tourists from Moscow. It's early afternoon,
on my watch 1:00 pm. No lunch today.
Finally, almost
soaked, we're welcomed – thank God, beneath
a roof – to his art-barn sanctuary (maybe there will be
hot coffee?) His witchcraft-lab – all the walls are
shelves filled with witchery! Teeny weeny paltry bones!
The bones of birds prepared with his Russian
wife Irina's help, probably – after their dinners
(dinner? – instead of aromatic coffee smell, the Northern
waves of Britten's music).
Unbelievable! – These
bones were a sculptor's sculptures – pluralize awakening

II

The witch-alchemist process? Sir Henry Moore nods, smiling –

'All my works come about through my
interest in bone forms. I use an ancient Greek Archimedes
lever – the simplest First Class Lever. One of my hands holds
(he demonstrates) a bone. Do you see the vertebra? The
other hand with the lever's small arm touches the bone.
The knife on the lever's other arm reflects
my motions & cuts the same shape from the
plastic foam, but an a larger scale. You see – a white
foam maquette of my future sculpture.'

Got it, readers? So simple, so effective. We were as excited as kids.
I'm back. In Moscow the same May, but the end.
The sun plays on the green branches & the breath-stopping lilac shrubs.
But I'm overwhelmed by English inspiration & Henry
Moore appears in my everyday tales.

O! An amazing coincidence! At this time in the seventies
the great sculptor donated 200 masterpieces
to the AGO, to the Art Gallery of Ontario.
Ontario? You know? In Toronto? Not Sorrento?
Or Toledo? AGO? Is it an abbreviation of Prado?
My knowledge of Canada went no farther than
Soviet-Canadian Hockey matches
O! I felt sorry for these orphans, my former English Much-Hadham
friends. My nightmare in my Moscow bed – these
stone guys blindly walk with their slow VIP gaits
through the dense Canadian forest, snapping
the wild dense age long maple trees & frightening
rich Canadian moose.

III.

A small World. In a new Millennium I meet
Sir Henry Moore again. I mean – his family
of sculptures. As the fates decree,
as I'm walking through the modern
downtown of Toronto, I see the bronze Archer at
Nathan Phillip Square – Moore's first visitor
from the sixties.
I go to the Ontario Art Gallery,
to the sculptor's largest collection in the world.
O! A happy encounter! I smile at these
clean groomed elegant clumsy fellows,
and they point willingly at their bird bone embryos
behind the museum glass. O! I'm happy!
I meet my youth! Thank you, Sir Henry Moore, for
your great generosity!
2008. November. O!
We have a great Event – the Grand Opening –
or landing – on Toronto ground – the avant-garde
glass-space Transformation of the AGO –
the new home saucer of the great Sir
Henry Moore's great alien children.

ICON

Amadeo's Sonnet to Anna

*A deception that elevates us
is dearer than a host of truth.*
— Marina Tsvetaeva

Your bright appearance in my boring being – Anna
Your gorgeous flex-curve's linear contours – Anna
Your face is an ideal of my painted women – Anna
Your strange alien words' murmuring range – Anna

You gave me an electric feeling with your snake-hands
With your thin wrists ringed with twinkle-bracelets
Gliding to your palm's transparent fingers
With the long flowers leaning against my chest

And your Venetian white mask blessed by your eyes –
Green in the morning like your green Black Sea,
Black in the night like the black veil of the Baltic
Powdered by St. Petersburg's unmelting snowflakes –

Your icon-look pale oblong is my sad prayer-pain – Anna
Your icon-image is my first love misfortune – Anna

JACKIE

'Isn't life a series of images that
change as they repeat themselves?'
— Andy Warhol

PART ONE

why do I dare to write about Jackie?
probably this weak connection
to the seventies, coming to Moscow the Mona Lisa
is a huge sensation, almost the October Revolution
armed red-star soldiers surround
the Renaissance First Lady
she's behind a thick armored glass cage
red velvet framed like Lenin in his Mausoleum
the church-jail's warm-yellow inner light
two million Soviet people in line

yes! probably this weak connection
a decade ago before the Giaconda's Russian crusade
Jackie's three-days-in-Paris official visit
"I'm the man who accompanied Jackie to Paris"
her husband's known joke
but his serious French deal with president de Gaulle
is a Soviet-rocket Russian-discussion
so Jackie's love for the Paris art of her Sorbonne
is done with culture-cultured Andre Malraux
during the journey of the Louvre's Giaconda

no gowns from the chic Givenchy
no Louis Vuitton shirts for John
and Jackie's lack of time for her soul-image maker
Oleg Cassini's design-prestige

but short shot shift ship-shipping
o yes! shot shift ship-shipping
ship a special cabin across the Pacific ocean
sphinx-smiling Mona-Lisa
nine French guards two Louvre officials
Giaconda-eyed da Vinci five hundred years watching
all watch over Mona Lisa's first voyage

hey! do you hear the SS sirens in Hudson harbour?
hey! move over!
Giaconda in Camelot! "blockbuster" for three months!
two million people! (with the same amount in Moscow!)
queued in Washington New York!
Jackie's deed-deal heroism for the New World's people
Jackie Jacqueline Lee Bouvier Kennedy
still not Onassis

PART TWO

I'm stuck to my black-white TV in Moscow
November 1963
Jacqueline Lee Bouvier Kennedy
(still not Onassis)
I see her mournful star-sad face
I cannot see her John
bang crack a fire shot
a gun went off with a loud bang
why do I dare to write about Jackie?
a heroine belonging to "one brief
shining moment that was known as Camelot?"
her words – the elegant First Lady floating above King Arthur's
round table in this far-off time the sixties
I lived in a different world

my Moscow peeping voyeur complex
like the ancient tailor Tom & his Lady Godiva
for me as a young man she seemed
just a stylish beauty-girl
o yes! with her beyond the clouds status-flight
alas I couldn't know
she was mad about poetry about art
about her own poems
I couldn't know
her flick-flip fillip photo job
her journal-journalism profession
Vogue Prix de Paris winner
I couldn't know

I couldn't know
her long shot of a Massachusetts
Senator's interview –
flick-flip fillip shot magazine-newspaper
and then her proud Ladyship
Jacqueline Lee Bouvier Kennedy
(still not Onassis)
the White House's mythical First Lady
I couldn't know
a Russian guy Oleg Cassini was Jackie's
image-maker & John-Jackie's friend
their thin-sophisticated guide
for their both refined & charismatic looks
but I know now
I have a Cassini tray from Toronto's
St. Lawrence Market Garage Sale
from an old rural owner for $2! o gosh!
this relic of the American Camelot of the 60s
is worth a couple thousand
furthermore –

I've bought Oleg Cassini's 'My Own Fashion'
book for 50 cents –
you know the Good-Will donation store
the final paradox of the Arthur Epoch
I know now I write this strange devoted
poem devoted to history
for my obsessed Saint-nothing cents
after a short grassy night

I'm in Toronto Canada
I'm stuck to my big screen
a TV commercial for the AGO July-October 2006
Andy Warhol Supernova
"Stars Death Disasters 1962-1964"
curated by Canadian filmmaker David Cronenberg
with his big lecture about Warhol's images

shot-shots image-photographs
a long shot static shot
of the sad funeral event
Jacke's strong celebrity-obsessed
art-friend the artist Warhol
pearl-silver silk-screen paintings blown up
of the assassination's chronicle
all on the wall
the famous many shots
Jackie's perfect but uneasy face
slight colour touches
among the celebrities of Warhol's vibrant art
the former but forever American First Lady's
sixteen images
Jacqueline Lee Bouvier Kennedy
Lady Onassis

KARENINA
> *'...someone's death always causes a kind of stupefaction...'*
> – Gustave Flaubert, Madam Bovary

O   paradox! Such a bright crispy fall but... O! My heart's beating!
My   gloomy spirits! I know now! He hurried to his bride!
Yes!   I know... our love was just his vanity! O! My long torment! I
know   what I need to do! I'll leave my car! O! It's hell...
but near   the subway! I won't let him make me... miserable.
O! Down!   Down! O! This bee-hive platform!
O rush hour!   My harsh rush! No way through! The dissolving noise!
vanished train!   I'm next! I'm squeezing to the edge!
The drawing-up   black mouth... my rescue's source!
This tunnel-throat   will light-ignite! the metal killer's eyes!
I cannot get my spot!   These stupid moving-standing people!
I missed my train again!   O finally! The proper place! my
guillotine! A cold metallic   heavy-breathing giant-iron! I shudder with
the crack-crush – my smash   -crashed skull! My burned brain!
The buried pavement-toss like a   stormy sea makes me sick! O this
crowd! This cheeky staring man!   This pseudo-stylish lady!
But all of them hurry to their homes   to their cold wives & husbands!
To their shaking nests! To their kids   these snotty nestlings!
 Kids? Kid? O kid! O! my Serozha!   O! Loving bird! My son!
"Mo-o-om!" O! Who cries? A neigbour   platform boy cries?
"Mom! The train! The train! It's coming!"   My third train? I hear
its noisy rhythm! Two spear-piercing monster   eyes... I see!
My urban brightly-lit grave! O! The ill-omened   racket! There!
Down! O! Push me, my grave-crowd! Again this   boy's voice!
O my Serozha, do not disturb my sin from my third   fate! My Trinity!
O Lord, forgive me everything! O my Serozha! Away   illusions!
I hate you, Alexei! My icy traitor! Away, second Alexei,   pale-handed
devil-spouse! A paradox... both Alexeis! A paradox that   I am here!
Not in my car! What am I doing? For what? O my Serozha!   No fear of
my mournful ruin! The fear of life! Oh no! I need to live! Not   sin!
Just sun! O sunny shiny son! I run to you! My dear! O Serozha!

LIBRARY

for Paris' new Landmark BNF established in 1368

1988 Mr. Mitterrand announced the construction
of architect Perrault's blast-concept – the French
memorabilia of 10 000 000 volumes with 4 (four)
100-metre see-through Pillars – for books   four

        vertical book-layers   heated by the   Sun-Soleil
        protected by   a complex high-tech   anti-glass
        put on the huge wood stair   square as a temple
        the guards – the roof-top's landing helicopters

it could fight with the monster Goliath who needs a
temple – who wants to grasp these   four tempting
temple lights to turn them   upside-down for using
as a holy sanctuary in the ancient   Greek tradition

        the temple's roof will be not a rough-light marble
        but   this podium's dry hard-wood – now the floor
        instead of a roof   an upstairs cornice of African
        wood and it's terrible!   I am not ancient Goliath

i like this Glass Crypt!   the over-light book-dream
with the underground   but over-green trees reading
place! I am not Goliath –   o! I like all of Paris' look
with the roof-mansards and this new Eco-Concept!

        away with Goliath's rebellion!   I drink the dense
        orange French romantic whirl-foam   coffee upon
        Mitterrand's four glass giants   at a small café of
        the modest dwelling aria, not the crowded Bercy!

MAYAKOVSKY

> *I like Mayakovsky on a step*
> *of cool marble.*
> — Frank O'Hara

Mayakovsky! I hear your voice from
my youth from my life and again from
my small flat computer — monumental & strong!
your Left-March — not right step! — don't lose step —
just left march! march! march! left!

'I like Mayakovsky on a step of cool marble' —
Frank O'Hara loved Mayakovsky Vladimir
in Russian… Vladimir-Vladimirovich
Russian Soviet Poet! American visitor!
the New World's   poetic discovery
of a full-fed
American   life
Mayakovsky   long sailing on his ship
with   his future   futurist prospect-perspective
his personal prospect — he had an American daughter
but he was the Soviet Passport holder
the Soviet Poet — first Russian performer — an avant-garde artist
the art-slogan posters' creator
the PUNK Verses' Beginner with his struggling heart
the built sculpted art figure — with his hand up!
toward the high restless sky with the CLOUDS!
left! left! left! left! left! left!
the poetic white CLOUDS —
not in the trousers — not in his hose
where is the proletarian *Passport*
the CLOUDS of slogans — he cries for New Life
but Revolution illusion delusion

    away from   the discovery of Revolution
    away   from an ocean ... away

from   the   sea-ship ... illusion-delusion

'love's   boat crushed' ...
his last poem's words of his boat of heart & of soul
his fan O'Hara seconding-echoing him decades later
'I embraced a cloud – but when I soared it rained'
a bitter illusion – delusion in life & in love
politics' illusion – love-feeling delusion the lonely soul
pulling his gun's trigger with the words – *'Lily – love me'* ...
Lily wrote Stalin ... asking permission
To publish great poetry by Mayakovsky
 'the best & the most talented poet of the Soviet Epoch' –
the second words – trigger of Stalin
o Mayakovsky! I hear your voice!

NUDE

for Bob Cooper

As I attended my Life-Draw Classes
"Who is the model?" I phone Bob Evening.
Scott answers "Peter" "Ah! Peter? Perfect!
He's anatomic, he's body-built & a God of Greece

Thursday 8:15! late fifteen minutes Why am I late?
"Timothy's" cups wait for a small Break
Graphite-coal-pencil pastel-sanguine Brush-pencil-pen
Squeak on the paper dirtying the White

Eyed-face, art-fingers, Bruce water- Colours
Bob's head is down his pencil brown As Leonardo's
He draws his children, sends them For Christmas
For Russian ears his fluent tongue's Da Vinci code

I touch an album, ten minutes pose With a lead-holder
Shading with fingers, old-fashioned Drawing
John's face El-Greco he takes Great photos
Still in Toronto star Robert Waters Cuts silhouettes

With plasticine Karl build-sculpts Peter
Precisely graceful, teeny-weeny Miniature
Time goes slowly – blithe Peter's Tired,
Shift-shivers, standing he smiles Confused.

A break is starting, the cup-lids Open
Kind Murray asks him "Bring you A coffee"?
"No!" a naked Peter holds a plastic Bottle
Drinks his cold water, I (near Peter) Drink my warm tea

OLIVER

>*I believe a leaf of grass is no less*
>*then the journey-work of the stars.*
>   – Walt Whitman

I am Oliver! – my friend
don't look at me like that! you look so anguished
why?
you've been here for six years? I for thirty-two
I am 32   I'm not   a townsman & like farm-life
why do horses have   no horns like buffalo?   I saw foxes'
traces when   I lived on my father's farm   he died I'm here
blind as a bat I fly   from barn to   this bar's beer's slur

               my favourite
                        Canadian Blue!   Oh!   Oh!
         my favourite Canadian bl… oh!   sorry! Bl…Blue!

I like talking to you   my mother stays with my older brother
I work for him   for my   older brother
heavy logs   light cold proof panels   veneer
I'm his auxiliary handy-man with back pain
it's why I came to talk   to you about my hard work
in spite of my back pain   oh… I… knock on wood I'm okay

                I'm not
                        a drunk   at… at all!
           o! I'm not a drunk at all!

I stay with my   new friend we have two bedrooms
because he can't stand   animals but   I have
two dogs my hairy friends   they sleep with me
they lick my beer lips   they remind me of   my

former farming life   my horse & sheep's   fine faint   smell
in the high barn with the   sunny ceiling   windy windows

       My friend!
          I'm   not a… a…drinker!
  I am   O-o-o-oliver ! o-o-o!

PICASSO

1

Santiago's archive said:
The great artist Pablo Picasso was baptized here in 1881
with the names – Pablo Diego José – Francisco de Paula –
Juan Nepomuceto – Maria de los Remedios – Copiano
de la Santisima – Trinidad Clito – then added his father's mother's
names Ruiz & Picasso – as per Spanish custom –

2

Picasso's mother said:
'If you are a soldier, you will become a General
If you are a monk, you will become the Pope'

3

Picasso said:
'Instead, I was a painter & become Picasso'

4

e.e. cummings said:
Picasso
you give us things
which
bulge: grunting lungs pumped full
of sharp thick mind
you hew form truly

5

Picasso's loving children said:
I'm Paulo; my mother is his first wife Olga Khokhlova
I'm Maia; my mother is Marie-Thérése Walter
I'm Claude; my mother is Francoise Gilot
I'm Paloma; my mother is Francoise Gilot

6

Sotheby's said:
Picasso's *Garson á la Pipe* sold for USD $ 104 million on May 3, 2006

QUADRUPLE

1			2
	a-b-C	D-e-f	
	g-h-F	J-k-i	
	alphabeT	Lexicon	
	words words wordS	Letters letters	
	a black squarE	Birth of art	
	autumn-winteR	Spring & summer	
	blowing winD	Flying birds	
	to the soutH	To the north	
	reflecteD	Mirrored	
	on the icE	On the water	
	harvest-weddinG	Concept-breeding	
	knock insidE	A crack in a shell	
	wait for lifE	A sharp beak	
	axis' lifE	Nature's axis	

3			4
	we are borN	We are dead	
	all of uS	Need somebody	
	we gave birtH	Joyful kid	
	our chilD	Has a mother	
	every fisH	Swims in water	
	every horsE	Eats the grass	
	our axeS	Circulate	
	a painting's axiS	A black square	
	music-axiS	Axis-verse	
	words words wordS	Letters letters	
	lexicoN	Alphabet	
	g-h-F	J-k-i	
	a-b-C	D-e-f	

79

REFLECTION
to Great Pushkin

Hey Monkey! – a Poet likes to say
Looking into the mirror at his reflection
The olive-black but red-haired Monkey
Looks at his apish smile
He combs his curly curls
Framing the long thin nose's oval
With an alert look staring strait ahead
A light & weightless jumping gate
With the sting-piques
Of wound-burning words
Walks jumping running
Then the brisk Monkey hangs on the nest-bough
Above the high society of Saint-Petersburg
Above the dancing ball looks down
And holds his Monkey's body
By his strong flexible long tail
By his bent hairy legs
For his free Monkey business
Grasps fingering
The passing crowd's heads
A scare-trick thinking
To awaken their justice fairness equity
The Monkey pinches bites laughing
The Monkey apishly sing-cries
In French without a Russian accent
In Russian without a French accent

SEVEN

to the Canadian Group of Seven with love

the march   of yellowing trembling leaves
the   blue sky   between torn clouds
the creeping wind   from the waving rippling lake
the lonely   boat softly   gliding on the water
         a dark figure   far off   on the sloping shore
         four seasons' nature of   this Canadian Group of Seven

the hunter Thompson   the heart   of the new fraternity
his life in forests was   a legend   with his canoe
1917 Tom Thompson   untimely   death in canoe lake
     drowning disappearing among his   framed scenic canvasses
         although his painted forests   were so transparent
         o! nobody could find trace of   him until   today

a couple of years later Thompson's seven friends   strengthened
founded   established   the Group of Seven   bell chiming
a virgin forest's fog   pure water's splash   a crystal ice's cold
uniquely Canadian environmental style   Seven amicable roads
the old world's descendant artists   captured a feeling of the nature
& Tom   Thompson remained   their slogan credo soul
&   their art's admiring artist   Emily Carr protective as a mother
hanging   in mid-air   her   painted scarf-twist above the Sevens

         the dark green   foliage-crowns spinning as an umbrella
         above the   woods & lakes & Thompson & all SEVENS
         Harris   McDonald Johnson Lismer Varley Carmichael

TRINITY

> *It's my lunch hour, so I go*
> *for a walk among the hum-coloured cabs.*
> – Frank O'Hara

I an walking
the first fall month breathes the summer farewell
not gloomy but with brisk sunny air already slightly chilly
it's lunch hour about noon & the running merry crowd
runs on the run or sits at the tables

I turn left too
the inviting glass of the Eaton Centre's roomy
atrium from festive Yonge Street to its shady flank
the different quiet world this isolated square the calm-faced
people no playful gaits I see the church of the Holy
Trinity with a café sharing the same brick-wall
the modest sign "Trinity Café" yes lunch

I enter
not crowded a few soup-salad eaters but
the café workers crowd are behind the counter & in the
open kitchen the coffee is slow moving
strange drawling precious pouring of soup into
deep bowls cleaning trays & tables saying to customers
"Good day" politely smiling

I look for soup
not fat not creamed skim-milked with a whole-wheat
bread slice plus margarine it is the proper place!
"three seventy-five" says Lesley Norton the café cashier
"we are not-for-profit we're from
the Mental Health Agency we help them to adapt

we have more workers than customers" while I eat
my healthy cream-purée a squinting man
says to me loudly "Good bye!"
the Trinity "three-seventy-five" world becomes
so close to me but not to this euphoric-blithe crowd

I spin among
the lunch-pedestrians with the slogans:
"eaters eat this holy low-fat eating! think of your
healthy lunch! think of your running souls! please
sometimes try to share with
Lesley Norton your lunch minutes! at 6 Trinity
Square Toronto ON M5G IBI!"

UNISON

I know it's early June   I'm in
a reanimation room after my surgery
my birthday's soon opening my eyes
I enter into   a swoon-frozen unison
I know it's early June   I'm in
a reanimation-room after my surgery
my birthday soon   opening my eyes
I enter into   a swoon frozen unison

through   the frozen ill eye glasses
not a living sound   dissonance
but some blurred-indistinct   unison
a bitter sweet harsh   unknown taste

unison   of slightly noisy technology
the unison   of white silhouettes
white piles   neighbours in this ward
a unison   of white blurry blue

a devilish devious   proposal
in unison with a   white vibrant view
of all ingratiating quiet noise   smell
Vladimir   would you like to shave?

o still not a nurse   a caring voice
just   a Procrust cold metal bed
I still feel   an after life suspend
a lukewarm foggy   foam brush

the unison   of a tickling scratches
cutting surgery again   then
I semi-see   a known face peering

who's seeking   the shaved beauty

I know it's early June   I'm in
a reanimation-room after my surgery
my birthday's soon opening my eyes
I enter into   a swoon frozen unison

VERDICT

> *...a dark wood where the straight way was lost.*
> – Dante Alighieri, *The Divine Comedy*

L: "Don't run from me on your wheelchair! I recognize you! I'll say to you all I've wanted for my whole life! Always you were my enemy!"
M: "Leave me alone, old woman!"

L: "We're peers! O! Our youth! O! *The Blue Angel!* You cross my road. It was my real chance! You cannot take away my Saint Martyr status now!"
M: "Are you Saint *Fuhrer's* protégé?"

L: "My *Fuhrer* was my friend! Not you! I hated your fox-face always! You seduced my Sternberg – like many years later 3 Kennedys!
M: "Don't envy me, a woman!"

L: " A damned multi-sinner! You sold your holy Heimat for songs for hostile soldiers! I fought for honest art! I say it as a German woman!"
M: "As a German Shepherd!"

L: "Shut up! Being a patriot is not a stigma! Long live my Heimat! My *Triumph of the Will!* Remember my soul filming waving banners?
M: "I didn't see your propaganda!"

L: "Your words are beyond measure! One of the Top Ten movies was my *Triumph!* Together with *October* of the monster Stalin's *Eisenstein!*"
M: "Russians did not burn people!"

L: "You're stubborn! You know I was a pariah for decades! After age 70 I plunged into the ocean filming Geography! Am I not a Martyr?!"
M: "Recall – Saint Peter is a Jew!"

WAR

> *... live for today, hope for tomorrow.*
> – Albert Einstein

The roll of a drum!	A trumpet blows!
                1940.
The air raids!	The Blitz!
            Coventry
the relic city of old Britain.   The chief of the
Luftwaffe unleashed a hundred & fifty bombs
from bases in Brittany   on this old town.
The Nazi raid mockingly   musically named
"Operation Moonlight   Sonata". The town
bombed cruelly. The 1000 year old historical
            Cathedral ruined.
The roll of a drum!	A trumpet blows
                1943.
The deciding   War-battle
            Stalingrad
not leaving a stone standing – the same with
Coventry Luftwaffe   dropping on Stalingrad
70 tones of War supplies   a day for months.
The momentous moment of the War crushed
stones melting metal   hold back your tear
            Stalingrad!
        The break of War
The roll of a drum!	A trumpet blows!
            Stalingrad!
The Nations'   Anti-Hitler Allies.
Nations cooperating   against an aggressor
            Stalingrad
                &
            Coventry

became   Twinned Brothers   forever.
The new Coventry Cathedral's Consecration
Mass
Requiem
by Britten.
A gigantic bronze Stalingrad Mother-Russia
with a raised sword memorializes the WWII
victims of the relative   Twinned Brothers
Coventry
&
Stalingrad
The roll of a drum!   A trumpet blows!

XIOPING

I enter the subway car
stand in front of the sliding door –
I need to get off soon

left of the door – a man is reading
right – a tall music-eared guy
looks for something in his cell
they do not stir

the door slides open
some people – a Chinese man
stops facing the door – I'm behind him
suddenly he whistles loudly
some Chinese melody –
o so loudly – muffling of the subway noise
this whistling rucksack-proud Chinese man

left of the door – a man is reading
right – tall music-eared guy
looks for something in his cell –
they do not stir

I was nervous
but I remembered another Chinese guy
my friend – the writer – Xiaoping
(who does not whistle loudly)
he gave me detailed information
about publishing – now so topical for me
o! I will call him – Xiaoping
the door slides – I think my whistler –
loudly whistling – he smiles at me
as a welcome – my stop is next

YOU

Quadruple Squares Poem

      o tell me   who are you
      a poet? the sky
      with the   rain snow hail
      or you're   the water ocean
      river?   the strong wind of
                       our feelings
      dying every time in stormy

air of the tangled   blast
imbroglios?   or flying in
the trembling paradise but
distant from our life? from
red sunset   or gold sunrise
are you a   quaking piano
chord of   your

      passionate sad parting with
      your virile calm
      restraint in the imprisoning
      autumn frame?
          are you a mutinous
      axis' trajectory   of a rainy
      swiftly running creek with a

flooding   flounder of
   memories with a sad
perpetual existence?
an incarnated   cosmic
element with songs in your
verse voice? o tell me who
are you a poet   ?

ZAHA

'I have won what? The Pritzker Prize?
Would you say that a second time?'
— Ms. Hadid's phone call

a new Art time came to the World to say goodbye to the
history of architecture's gravity to the Pole-Beam
structures in construction to column frieze architrave! now
new physical rules chime! forget gravity! greet the balance
of dynamic substance! the cosmos fantasy of Art Designers!
along with the Diva the Baghdad Iraqi born ZAHA
HADID an architect absorbed in Asian Muslim & Western European
Culture & filled with the festive green blue mosaic mosques!
she came to London in the 70s to conquer the Euclid Parallels
Einstein's Relativity laws to turn the false last Art
Post-Modernism toward an honest abstract Deconstructivism
or Deconstruction digging through the past of art history .
I was greatly influenced by early Russian abstract artists,
mainly Malevich & El Lissitsky applying this to my architecture
Z A H A with her child like character of genius became a
non-British Avant-Garde Art Lady flying up to Anti-Gravity
to her Bird-Beaked Sky Scale Design with the flooding
parallel unparallel wall roof skin with her adolescent curiosity
in a fish eye perspective for our temple ache & dizzy heads!
o! her zero gravity *"Paper Architecture"*! BUT TODAY
SHE – ZAHA – flies already spanning our Globe with a long
line of her becoming REAL built whirl Symphonies – in Dubai
in Germany – Japan – US – Italy Hong Kong! o Great Lady!

I open a new Global & Mail paper o! Zaha enters our territory!
welcome to Canada! we'll meet you at designing of a residential
building on Front street! Hurrah! you're here! your road to Toronto
paved by your Co Cosmic Pilots Libeskind's Prism Crystal ROM
and Gehry's Gallery glass UFO of Transformation AGO!

PART III.

One touch of nature makes the whole world kin.
– William Shakespeare

THE EARLY MORNING SUN

> *Kisses can kiss us.*
> — Gertrude Stein

the early morning sun drinks the cold dew
from the meadow grass –
but the trembling distance between my kind
new-chosen Kiss-Kind Someone & my striving mind
shrinks very slowly –
in spite of my very zealous pilgrimage
to the Kind-Someone's tempting Land

I stand tiptoeing watching the summer
dense grass food field
filled with harmless being-inhabitants
feeding on the fresh ripe green meadow flesh –
the black-white cows in the meadow
so kindly seductive like
my Kind-Someone's figure in this landscape

I see my Kind-Someone's closeness
lit by the low sun
with running-toward-me inviting features
the captivating lips keep
the magic flute of morning musically playing
melody streaming above the green meadow

o! I really know I'll run
into the crooked dangerous
high grass bull-cow magnetic moist meadow –
well known but unknown
hidden snakes & broken glass beneath the grass
with my waltz turns converted into salt pillars –

WHO'S AFRAID OF MY PLANTS ?

> *'The eyes of others our prison;*
> *their thoughts our cages.'*
> — Virginia Woolf

who afraid of my plants?
these three trees –
huge mutinous house-grown plants
grew by my shady window so quickly
closing my narrow backward view-panorama
they were brought a few years ago
teeny-weeny grassy sprout-shoots
in small plastic bowls from Wal-Mart or Good-Will
by my odd-mutinous acquaintance
my dubious restless but good Samaritan guy Nick
he came with these green weak blind puppies
then – he bought the huge clay dishes
Nick's kids were growing speedily cheeky green
their quick temper's tempi was going
from Nick's naturalist tempo-nature
who had a soul of some Bestiary's rank
loving silent room-inhabitants
he said – his dead kind agro-father
had many house-plants –
but Nick owned also a flat glass-walled aquarium
with vertically swimming coloured fish
I praised his mystery interior and I've got
these kid-plants which became trees

who is afraid of them – of my huge house-plants?
I am –
I am afraid of my thick fleshy deep-green plants

such a fishy
busy crazy business – run-blowing
money or some free-money occupation Nick had –
this good notorious Samaritan guy Nick
with a balance unbalanced
on the sharp-cutting edge of many habits
buying selling? – what? – the puzzle's what
Madonna-Bjork tickets' brave-blind buyer-seller
or marijuana & native cigarettes
the risky expert of E-Bay sales
from the unisex underwear to fancy sex toys
construction? o yes! – upgraded
renovated for good – but for selling –
I'm not sure for good – but for his buy-selling activities

who is afraid of them – of my huge plants?
I am –
I am afraid of my thick fleshy deep-green plants!
I told you
Nick buy-sells life's bio-info because he is
my mystic plants' creator
I do not know where Nick is now –
in a jail? or in a different country?
probably in Mexico? or something else?
I feel that
my speedily growing plants are following
their author in their habits
I've never been a house-planter
plants couldn't live at any of my former homes
neither in this country nor in the former one
at first I felt embarrassed
I'm waiting for the untimely death of these
newborn poor thin grassy future giants (?!)
I watered them twice a week

and I was so sorry about my shady room
some days they put down their weak heads
and look at me kid-sorrowfully
as though saying their farewell
but life continued for my young kid-tenants
and I lived in parallel I was getting older
they were growing up

who is afraid of them – of my green house plants?
I am –
I am afraid of my thick fleshy deep-green plants!

days weeks
months years passed by –
my good Samaritan Nick slowly disappeared
my plant-plantation was growing
tall huge strong beefy and boisterously green
exhaling their chlorophyll for the intimacy
of our close relationship through our common air
nobody is at my suite-place –
just myself – their breadwinner
and they – breed-drinkers –
look out the shady window & also –
as I watch by chance –
they stealth-watch curiously my steps
and follow my traces
lightly rustling their limp leaf-hands
without usual house-plants' polite conventions
no sun from outside for joy – just shade-shadow mystery
for their dark secret –
inherited from Nick's green-easy life
I slept for
many years in my small bedroom
behind the open sliding glass wall

I guessed – my tenants could be lunatic night-walkers
my mad-insane presumption
I felt some suspense-thrill
the fool-trees tease & smile behind my back
but they are shy by day – waiting for night
my deep dream-sleeping

who is afraid of them – of my huge leaf-plants?
I am –
I am afraid of my thick fleshy deep-green plants!

I turn off
my lamp I close my eyes
confirm the dark coziness – then – then –
then I hear the light sliding noise
of the plants' moving bowl-pots
probably they're exercising
elbowing past the dense room furniture in the dark
and they are – closer – closer –
I feel the slightly-windy waves
of the giant fan's Schefflera umbrella-leaves
the Lotus-Bamboo sticks pinch my pajamas
the Spathiphyllum strokes my hot cheeks
I'm afraid to open my eyes
but I open
nothing – nobody – probably they ran away fast
so agile & so sporty
standing up
I see them slightly shaking after their voyage
my green friends – my enemies – my house plants
they smile into the dark backyard watching
the silhouette of a tall & long vague building
I go back
I close the bedroom glass
digital red showed me Three AM

I need to sleep before my busy day –
o my God or Hell!
a loud crazy knock on my closed glass-wall!
jarring jingling tinkling knock-knocking
the revolutionary terrorists make this revolution
o my! the alarm! o! my poor neigbours!
what is wanted by these innocent fool house plants?
why their thunderstorm? I need to call their parent
that guy Nick – the trouble-making reason?
o yes! I heard his – Nick's – electronic-bell jail-fetters
the hidden iron-ring cries behind my glass:
Vladimir open! open! or call me! phone me!
or I'll break your door!
sorry! I did not know the jail's phone-number!
but open – I'm afraid!

who is afraid of them – of my huge leaf-plants?
I am –
I am afraid of my green plants & Nick's door-knock !

the scary noise
awakens me & my scared open eyes see
the red digits – already Seven AM
it's time to water my trees – today is Wednesday
and to go about my business
produce the hiss-fizzing coffee smell
splash the splashing shower-water
my day-trees wait patiently
for their huge morning drink – they know –
it will be after my morning coffee

who is afraid of them – of my huge leaf-plants?
I am –
I am afraid of my thick fleshy deep-green plants!

O HARE!

O HARE! My Boy! – they all say you're a Playboy!
    This is not your fear
Your real fear is being HERE in time for Easter.
    Don't show us your short shaking tail
Blond females have your long Ears
    To hear – o HARE! – you as a Tickle-Tricky Male
Playmates look at your long Ears, o Hare!
    And they'd like to have your painted Eggs for Easter
And they love you as a manly Gentleman!

O RABBIT RABBIT

O Rabbit Rabbit
    I meet you with a whole basket of fresh apples
You are a model for a proper married couple
    Under the Sun
With so many daughters & many sons
    For me you are an expert of the home
And an ability for shopping
    Teach me your smart family wisdom
O Rabbit Rabbit
    I must wear my house slippers
And come to my lost family for supper

THE FLY SLEEPS

The Fly sleeps in the cold winter
      Yielding its air-space to a "Winter Snow Fly"
The cold winter goes & then a warm sunny Spring
      The Fly-flakes drop melt
Transform into waltz-spinning flying Flies
      The Fly again revives
Buzz-joy dance-singing
      But I cannot melt my ice
Like long ago
      In my many past Springs

THE MICE

The Mice
        The little Mice
There is much food in your tight holes
        But outside
It's still so soft & warm
        But just at night
It is already cold for you
        The little Mouse-guys
Like you
        The running mice
My running days
        Always
They are so quickly running
        I cannot catch them
These hurrying mouse-guys
        One more again
To use them twice

OCTOPUS STOP!

Octopus stop! You can be inked by my hand-pens
        Or read my salt-water-written poetry essay
Be careful don't step on my long leg-hand-limbs
        Or better stay away
From my eight legs from my walk-way
        I am the God's respectable creature
With many palms – hand-leg's pen-holders
        Respect me and look over my essay

MEDUSA YOU ARE A DEVIL!

Medusa you are a Devil! don't scare me & don't glue my legs
    With your wet purple sticky glue
Wandering in your fresh or salty sea water
    Sticky Jellyfish
Allow me to move & breath air
    I beg
As our Lord promised me
    Without fear.

O OX!

O ox! O my dear and puzzling friend
    Your trembling nostrils
Are so wet tempting and so glassy-warm;
    At the same time
So dangerous are your sharp horns
    My thick-headed tempting Monster
With your breath-tempting nostrils!

THE HOME SPHINX

The home Sphinx
      You like or love me
You are proud to wait for me always
      For me
Your loving master
      You are my loving Cat
The sign of our home
      And our proud honor.
You have to study the passing Cat's significant gait
      So graciously
Especially if you sense a mouse
      You object?
"You mean – the Cat catches the mice?
      Not now
The Cat just waits for them."

PEACOCK IS LIFTING

Peacock is lifting the shining green-blue tail up
                                           To the sky
This gigantic fan-plumage
                    Of sweet poetry
                                    Proudly boasts
The crowned Queen-Bird doesn't fly
                    No Wing Flap,
The South-Oriental Queen-Tsarina just walks
       This beauty knows
If she flies
               Her beauty will be lost

MY WINGED PEGASUS

My winged Pegasus spin-flew
        Over Mount Olympus
With his poetic Muse
        And he gave me a sparkling Drink
For my inspiration
        From his Horse Water Spring
For my orphan poems' light creation
        But my Pegasus galloped off
To fight with the Chimera & Amazons
        And he forgot to give me
The oats of my work-energy's temptation.

PARISIAN FLEA

Parisian flea – o my sporty ballerina
        Hop-leap-quick-jumper!
You've been very close to many
        Hairy beasts
Since ancient times
        O please mark it!
Today is Sunday
        Flea, fly! Flea fly!
Hurry Flea! Do not miss
        A meeting with
Your many close & hairy friends
        At the Parisian Flea Market.

O WATER-BEING-CLONE

O Water-Being-Clone o Fish o Crab
      You are a Sage Wise Man
You found for yourself a Magic Stone
      You – if you want – move backward
To your Youth or many happy days
      You can see Wilde's Dorian always
In the mirror
      Instead of Mephistopheles' face
You can return to yourself fast
      As young researcher Faust
To your Gretchen
      O Crab! You are so smart!
Teach me your Backward-Art

YOU DOVE

You Dove were a postal flying messenger
        For early Christians
A letter written not with goose-quill
        But with your marble feather
Now we
        Post-Christians
Live very close together
        With electronic air
E-mail phone radio
        O Dove
O atavistic postman
        Now you are our sign of Peace
After Picasso's Doves
        We feed you and your crowd
In the square of Rome or Venice
        Or Toronto

HEY SIRENS

Hey Sirens in the stormy sea!
    The lighthouse light
The sailors' monstrous sailing plight
    The fierce fire eyed
Winged phantom-girls wandering around
    With the sinister singing sound
Smashed or crushed on the reef iceberg ground
    The Argonauts' ship with the Golden Fleece
Don't do it! the fire-eyed Sirens!
    The daughters of ancient mythic Greece!

BEAR IN THE FOREST

      Bear in the forest
Kind God's & dense wood's Creature
      You are upright – a real Man
You like to stay this way
      To show your high hairy figure
With your manly nippled chest
      Licking from your lips
A golden sweet yellow honey
      And in the forest you can't be missed
A hospitable soft host-crony
      A shaggy clumsy beast
But when you're teased – – –
      Fate is unpredictable & cruel
You could be called
      To a Man-to-Man forest duel
And by your mate-hikers missed

QUICKLY RUNNING LION

Quickly running Lion
      The proud King
Of noble furry golden color
      O King!
Hasten, run along the sandy hot Savannah!
      Hunters hurry to bring
The metal cage
      For you.
Instead of your King-throne
      Run
Manly King
      Alas
Your Kingdom is a fog-mirage
      A fading Fata-Morgana.

THE SERPENT COMES

The Serpent came
      To Eve
To bring the red-green Apple
      To show this round & perfect shape
To look at the live bright Apple's cheeks
      And embrace Adam's appled neck
To taste
      To bite
To show Adam this Apple
      To mock him

For her a first Lady's mockery

      Then the Serpent comes
To Adam –
      With tempting hissing talk
Shocked Adam grasps the unbitten Apple –

      No start no end no moral
For our sinful life

A PLAIN STRAY DOG NAMED LAIKA

a plain stray dog named Laika
        in Russian this means Barking Dog
half a century ago
        this was the first living creature on Earth
to fly into endless space
        half a century ago!
now in Moscow venerable grey-haired academics
        lay flowers at a monument unveiled
on the eve of Cosmonauts' Day
        depicting the agile good-natured Dog
strapped into a dissected Vostok rocket
        April 12 1961
Soviet pilot Yuri Gagarin follows the dog
        but long before Gagarin's flight
the Barking Dog Laika
        successfully blasted off into the cosmos
on November 3 1957 proving
        that a living creature could survive
being launched so high & experiencing weightlessness
        Laika was trained for eight months
including in a centrifuge & in a pressure chamber
        and died during her heroic historical flight
fighting for Russia in the space race
        the US space-program relied
on tests with primates
        protégé of Bestiary lover Darwin
the Russians say:
        "Monkeys are very ill-mannered –
they try to grab whatever they can
        they fancy they can switch whatever they like
but the Dog is a Friend of humans and

LIKE HUMAN COMMUTERS

like human commuters the Moscow strays
        travel on the Subway
waiting patiently for a train to pull in and
        its doors to slide open
they curl up on empty seats
        nuzzling their neighbours lounging in stations
outside strays have learned to cross
        the street with Muscovites
they wait for a green light
        but strays like all dogs are colourblind
researchers theorize they recognize the shape
        of the walk signal
strays form Moscow's character
        they have joined the street-beggars
the avid canine skills developed innovative strategies
        a big dog pads up silently behind a man
eating on the street and barks for his food
        then the dog eats it
the dogs don't have a lean and hungry look
        many Moscovites feed the strays & even
collected money to erect a bronze statue
        near the Subway for the abused strays
the strays' population is at about 26,000
        these friends of human-beings need food
they demand it from their elder brothers
        and make occasional attacks on Muscovites
a man was killed by a pack of strays
        living in a rambling and overgrown park
the strays aggressively defend their territory
        so scary to walk along a street at night
one is accompanied by the hungry pack of strays
        meanwhile in the Subway dogs nap

and one of them rises wanders a few steps
        to some discarded potatoes sniffs nibbles
then goes back to sleep in the Metro passage
        there will be better food later
the dogs know Muscovite life better than they
        know their fellow stray dog's life

I STARTED EARLY

I started Early – took my Dog –
  – Emily Dickinson

THE FIRST POEM

I started Early – took my master
A Poet – he is a Man
I am a Dog – he'd like a coffee
I'd like more meat

He is so strange – my Master-Poet
He's like a puppy – he is my Pet
He calls his Friend – I hear him smiling
"I started Early – took my Dog"

I took him – we're already Walking
We cross the Street – I lead the Way
My owner follows my shortened Route
Queen – Beverly – then Richmond Street

We are at my or our loving Store
I like the Morning sunny patch on the
Standing Solders – many Rows of Books
I smell these multi-scented Works

"I started Early – took my Dog –"
I hear his voice again – I am okay –
But my Dog's comfort I have Not
Because of his long Leash-Commands –

My Neck is round-squeezed
I'm a Dog – I am not a beaded girl

(I'd like proudly to say – I am a Male)
Alas – His Leash is my Reality

THE SECOND POEM

I lead my Master – Up-Escalator-lifted
He needs again a Coffee – here –
At a top-floor Starbucks – he forgets his Poetry
His memory needs a bold Cup

"I started Early – took my Dog –"
I hear again – o my! I lay! I'm here!
I hear his coffee chat in my Sleep-Nap –
I dream of my home – where he lives also

Then – Books Books – so many Books
The time approaches the day-end
To go Down – my extreme Anxiety –
The tech-electric-steps – ride-going Down –

I hate this Monster – the down-Escalator
I hate my extreme down-pull footsteps
A pulling-neck Lead – my Master-Monster
An invitation to my Fear-Beheading –

I Squat – for my resist-attempt
I Bend my shapely hairy legs
I Touch my tide-white Under-Tail
To the moving dirty metal steps

Already I calm-down – no Worry! –
No Disgrace! – I cannot Lift my leg!
He won – by his Pet-Stubbornness –
He spits – at my scared-vomit Feeling –

THE THIRD POEM

My going Down with my semi-Faint –
And my subconscious Dog Role
Continues – a Proud Elegant Pretence –
Supposedly – I guide him – Graciously

My nonplussed helpless Poet-Pet!
Let him display his sad descending!
Ouch! again a pull! – oh devil!
But I can tell – he's Tired

It doesn't bother me – I keep my proud Mask on
I go Down but my Dog's head is Up!
I know – Aristotle's words –
"There is honor in being a Dog!"

"I started Early – took my Dog"
Those are not Aristotle's words –
Yes – he took me – but with Emily Dickinson's
Romantic Words – about her & myself

No patience! – turn off your Cell –
It is Lunch-Time – we both started Early –
You took your Dog – I took my Poet-Pet –"
I Yelp & Pull – to the Subway nearby

I started Early – took my master
My master-owner – my Poet-Pet
I am a guiding Dog – he is a writing Poet
He needs a coffee – I need some meat

BEHIND THE DOOR

Behind the doors
He she it you I cannot see
so many doors he she it you
i see them passing the long walls outside
walking along a long corridor inside
door door door again a door
the mostly closed locked doors
these spaces' closed eyes
we cannot see the hidden ant-hill
the caged survivors
the holy kind smiling singles
or happy couples
or monsters & she-tigers
we cannot see
the tossing lady in her isolated room
all of us hear nothing
no crying & no scolding
she tosses lonely & is naked
behind the door
just a diamond ring on her finger
and her non-stop thoughts
run through her racing mind
behind the firmly closed door
nobody sees
nobody wants to use
but there is a peep-hole
o! no more peeping Tom
and nobody knows
the happy next-door cat
lies sleeping with its eyes closed
yawning sweetly
enjoying its loneliness

stretching its limbs with hidden claws
or showing its peaceful paws quietly
so quiet behind the door in the corridor
just a key's noise in the next door
o! it is the lady's key
really? o! no! so sorry! it's just a dream
of a sleeping cat next-door
so it is his own scenario
after its fresh flesh fish lunch alone
behind the door

THE MAN DIED

the Man died – but his Watch
        is still alive – although
it hides in the deep Grave
        the Watch works well – really well
it's ready to be laid on a live wrist
        the Bird flies randomly
above the dead man's Grave
        and finds this dense-grassy hidden Grave
and grasps from the dug-down wet-soil Grave
        this metal Wrist of the dead Man
the Watch is sharp-strong working
        and as an alive heart beat-ticking very loud
the Bird holds the Watch in its tacky beak
        this shining live part-organ of the dead Man
the well-working Wrist-Watch
        from the dug-out already empty Grave
no Man –
        no full rich mysterious dark Grave
but the well-ticking metal Watch
        works like clockwork
it's sticky-ticking – it's going well
        the Bird holds the Watch in its tacky Beak
the Wrist-Watch is really ready to tightly embrace
        the new Man's manly hairy Hand
the Bird still watches – waits with its present
        the Bird hurries to give somebody the Watch –
don't miss this Bird –
        the flying Bird still watches attentive diligent –
for the Story's End

THE HEAT

the heat of the hot summer day
        today we're in a small town
the slowly walking cars
        the crawling men & women
along the narrow motionlessly hanging streets
        some sleeping animals
a cat dead of its sweaty boredom

lies outside a stuffy house
        a bored owner holding a waving
paper behind the lowered blind
        of the sleeping house-face
with sleeping window-eyes
        like the eyes of the let-in cat
do not disturb this dream

this summer frozen afternoon siesta
        goes its own way
to the next face of the living
        not-sleeping house
o! the open window-eyes
        with a widely open door or mouth
not laughing but shouting

a loud sound like spitting outside
        instead of a barking dog
maybe due to the heat deep sleeping
        for your tired lazy ear this cut
blasting ungraciously
        radio-tape-music-rhythm
really unsatisfied or offended

why? probably that you
        did not buy something
did not drink its thin-washy coffee
        did not even look at the face-menu
therefore look at the next facade
        it will be a small town church
which will cool your soul

A KNOCK

a knock among a sharp midnight.
      12:00 am on my watch. I'm not home.
I'm outside – a sometime night street
      Inhabitant – a deep night.
sleepily dragging, tired,
      through my sleep-walking haze –
a rhythmic knock – two stones knock,
      loudly-bluntly rhythmically – tap-tap-tap.
a woman knocks – I've heard
      it for years – she sits on the asphalt –
knocking with a piece of asphalt
      on a granite building's base.
King-Yonge – my intersection.
      Embarrassed – I pass her every day –
she doesn't talk.
      she – tap-tap-tap – just knocks
she changed her customs.
      before, she smoked.
not knocked. She smoked.
      like a stylish lady, smoked.
in a stylish lady-smoking-room –
      artistically – wearing
a brimmed hat, – she smoked.
      now she – tap-tap-tap – knocks
the uniformed night-people give her
      steamy food in foil, steamy coffee
she neatly opens the silver foil –
      a faint smell & her noble manners.
12:10 – my lobby the elevator doors close
      12:30 am – my pajamas I open my night window
o! I hear with my decaf hot cup
      this knock again. o tap, tap, tap –

TWO WHITE-GREY BIRDS

two white-grey birds
        asphalt-walkers
these ruffled pigeons
        bump into each other
with stubborn-ox foreheads
        above the lion-fuzzy
aggressive collars – signs of war,
        strong-fighting or
strong-embracing
        their thin-prickly beaks –
pecking or
        kissing
a battle or
        a marriage-dance
transforms them into a united
        flapping four-winged
sphere-creature – a tiny Dutch
        windmill
a homeless man
        throws them a biscuit
distracts the shaking feathery ball of
        wrestlers or lovers –
from their cockfight or wedding
        afterwards
they tread along the asphalt
        as usual
two self-sufficient walkers
        both nodding
their smooth-round heads –
        to the rhythm of asphalt-walking
in both beaks pieces of
        biscuit

THE UNIVERSE SEEMS BANKRUPT

*The universe seems bankrupt as soon as we
begin to discuss the characters of individuals.*
– Henry David Thoreau

the universe seems bankrupt – as soon as we
begin discussing the character of individuals
who do not run into woods – but lie on sidewalks

in the very early morning – but my door
shuts loudly – I shudder – because –
all are still sleeping but I go out – I'm outside
a lingering long night – the weak grey-lilac light
the soft melt-falling flakes of snow – –
no walkers – quiet empty
the stopping sigh of glass-eye-sight
of the high-stone walls' dream still from the night
the pavement's snow layer is so white
but if I looked behind –
I'd see my rubber shoes' ribbed imprint
from my habitual moon-slow sticky steps –
my whisper-rhyme – of endless time
why? why am I wandering? why?
why did I close my home's door?
am I claustrophobic? no – I do not fear
my tight room-shelter –
I'm not scared but I don't like the noise of mats
I really like my high universal weightlessness –
my freedom – so spacious outside – with my
granite curbstone seat-throne for day & night
with shining metal backs jingle-falling
into my cup – still empty now
like for me my empty not-missing home

no angry or embarrassing next-doors
no painful pout-wincing – my wife-not-wife
no more her lying dog's reproachful eyes –
I close the door – it's close to zero –
I feel the spring – my morning lilac-light
"no nostalgia? – no return?" – quite right!

the universe seems bankrupt – as soon as we
begin discussing the character of individuals
who do not run into woods – but lie on sidewalks

NO BIRDS

no birds rain again
        inside me as a pain
I lean against the frame
        I look at sad splashes

no birds in the dense forest rain
        the road is clay no way
the tearing branch & bough
        drop their tears into puddles

no birds on the poor pouring trees
        the rustling noise of leaves
and birds are neatly hidden
        in the endless rain

no birds just rainy rain insane
        my own tears are also rain

FLYING AWAY

flying away from your their
spring source birth place
the quick short long slow
sounds signal – our words
these minds transmit messages
bio-physic oscillations
good shots to any membrane
absorbed by any listening sponge
reflected in mirror eyes
or simply leap on a stubborn hard surface
o shot flying waves
you are our essence & existence
although you are disappearing birds
in the boundless atmosphere
in the blue sky transparent air
deaf rays wave for elbowroom

I WATCH A BIRTH OF SONG

I watch a birth of song in sky
the flapping wings of birds
in the branches nesting –
they want to fly but wait for a
signal of the wing's wind
sharply waving their wings
creating the noise-hung echo
of the dry rustling spring smiling
noise flapping music silhouette
giving birth the loud blowing air waves
melodically sound rhythmically shine
a chilly fresh-breath aching tune
above the brown naked earth
sonorously lonely reflection of sound
the wings of wind the wind of wings
in the late no-snow melt-winter sprung
the nearly early still-imagined spring
a wind's deep inhalation sighs
above the curled shrubs' obstacle
climbs upon the tree shaking webs
birth of a bird wave wing song

THE MONOTONIOUSLY WIDE FRAMES
for my Mongolia trip

The monotonously wide frames
Of the running view from the car
The gap between Darkchan & Ylan-Bator
The endless space of the dense orange
Screwed up Mongolian wide-screen sunset
Along a primordial blank
A scene of red Mars scenery

The close-to-cosmic rarefied air
Of the empty vertical hanging sky
With the high motionless birds hung
Above the geometric computer-generated
Identical waves of hills stream along the
Shaved grassy flat
To reach the distant horizon

To call a monstrous darkness
The red yellow boom rings in my ears
The deafening stopped silence
Of Mongolia – a special planet
Of this wild uninhabited flat space
Free hands up like two wings
Of the sharp-sighted hanging birds

Watching the rare wanderers
The steppe-Bestiarian inhabitants
They're winged or wingless wonders
Like the large lonely horse & camel
The legendary saiga herd or sheep flock
Or jumper-runners – the agile gnawers
No trace of human life – is it a human earth?

The licked-by-endlessness
Slope shaping waving relief
Millions of years ago mountains leveled
Into the waving plain – no roads at all
But all this flat space is real
A very smooth self-governing communication
At the end of the 20th Century

We wait for the automobiles' motion
Oops! our car stopped! We're stunned – two men
Dead-silent sit on the ground – opposite each
Other with their stiff hands stretched ahead
Their high-booted legs motionlessly frozen
Two camel-horsemen auto-drivers
Bumped in this Galaxy's extensive freedom

They're two allied Pagan gods
Two new born-by-accident Buddhas sculpted
With their two stopped craft-vessels
Iron-face to iron-face
Such a strong desire they have
To find each other & kiss their
Blind & broken metal beasts

By chance am I an onlooker of the
Precisely arranged cosmos contact?
Or also a participant of this mythic deed?
I am not sure what the miracle is
The free hands up as new wings
Like a steppe sharp sighted bird
In the high tight sky that's getting darker

I feel I'm an ancient steppe Scythian

Sitting in my bloody oncoming alliance
Feeling in my unaccustomed backside-seat
This hard rude shaved grass wild eternal
Bed bottom of the million-year-old
Trace of glaciers beneath the vertically
Hang darkening red sky suspense

THE FROSTY SKY
for my Mongloia trip

The frosty sky the crispy sigh
Of rose white blue snow
Around the sliding ice
Perforated by so many holes
Made by the drills of my friends
These fishermen
Who enjoy the caught fish pile-dance
the eyed twist coil dancing tails
The eyes & tails small-sized or not
The waving gazing beasts
With their dreamy back diving
Into any of these many
Narrow icy holes
My craftsman-manly friends
Continue to pull these many-eyed
Tailed swimmer beasts
From the cold-icy round holes
And add a twisting dancing corpse
To the waving pile
My joy's restricted & I smile
As I feel my hunting failure
My fishing-rod my hook
Is empty of the twist beast's joy
My kind friend craftsmen laugh
The sky is slowly covered
By the cold rose grey early evening blank
The live corpse-de-ballet pile
Is honestly divided into four parts
The men laugh joyfully they'll bring
All the parts to their wives
"We'll come to you to help you eat!
Too much for your small single table!"

NOTES AND ACKNOWLEDGEMENTS

This compilation is a selection of poems that relate in one way or another to my move from Moscow to Toronto. Not only have I learned many things about my new home, but I also learned (and continue to learn) the English language and its great literature, including many poetic traditions. These shifting experiences have shown me how one culture can compliment so many others.

Many thanks to poet Jay MillAr for his great help and guidance through the world of Canadian poetry, and for his help in the editing and publishing of this book.

Thanks to my friends at George Brown College for encouragement with my poetry: poet Maureen Hynes, and professors Bill Knox, Luis Eisen, and Heather Rappaport.

Thanks to my young creative friends Angela Zito and Jon Apgar.

Thanks to staff of the Art Gallery of Ontario for their attention with my interest in Canadian art, especially to curator Maia Mari Sutnik.

And finally, thanks to my friend, Moscow architect Kirill Archipov, who was the first reader of many of these poems and a long-time supporter of my writing.

ABOUT THE AUTHOR

Vladimir Azarov is an architect originally from Moscow. His other books include *Graphics of Life, Black Square, My Bestiary,* and *26: Letters Poems Pictures.* Mr. Azarov lives in Toronto.